Paul Farley The Ice Age

PICADOR

First published 2002 by Picador
an imprint of Pan Macmillan Ltd
Pan Macmillan, 20 New Wharf Road, London N1 9RR
Basingstoke and Oxford
Associated companies throughout the world
www.panmacmillan.com

ISBN 0 330 48453 2

9 8 7 6 5 4 3

A CIP catalogue record for this book is available from
the British Library.

Typeset in 10/14.5pt Minion
Printed and bound in Great Britain by
Mackays of Chatham plc, Chath

This book is for Leila and Rafaela

Acknowledgements

Some of these poems have appeared in *Areté*, boomeranguk.com, the *London Review of Books*, *Metre*, *Poetry Review*, *The Printer's Devil* and the *Times Literary Supplement*. 'Diary Moon' and 'An Erratic' were first broadcast on BBC radio's *Night Waves* and *Front Row* respectively. 'Thorns' has been published as part of the CD catalogue that accompanied the exhibition *Republic of Thorns* (Wordsworth Trust, 2001).

Thanks are also due to the Arts Council of England for a Writer's Award in 2000; to the Society of Authors and the Royal Literary Fund for their timely help and support; and to Dr Robert Woof, my host during an eventful stay at Grasmere.

P.F.

Contents

The Ice Age

From a Weekend First

One for the money. Arrangements in green and grey
from the window of an empty dining-car.
No takers for this Burgundy today
apart from me. I'll raise a weighted stem
to my homeland scattering by, be grateful for
these easy-on-the-eye, Army & Navy
surplus camouflage colours that seem
to mask all trace of life and industry;

a draft for the hidden dead, our forefathers,
the landfills of the mind where they turned in
with the plush and orange peel of yesteryear,
used up and entertained and put to bed
at last; to this view where everything seems to turn
on the middle distance. Crematoria, multiplex
way stations in the form of big sheds
that house their promises of goods and sex;

to the promise of a university town,
its spires and playing fields. No border guards
will board at this station, no shakedown
relieve me of papers or contraband:
this is *England*. Nobody will pull the cord
on these thoughts, though the cutlery and glasses
set for dinner are tinkling at a bend,
a carriage full of ghosts taking their places.

Now drink to slow outskirts, the colour wheels
of fifty years collected in windows;
to worlds of interiors, to credit deals
with nothing to pay until next year, postcodes
where water hardens, then softens, where rows
of streetlights become the dominant motif
as day drains, and I see myself transposed
into the dark, lifting my glass. Belief

is one thing, though the dead have none of it.
What would they make of me? This pinot noir
on my expenses, time enough to write
this on a Virgin antimacassar –
the miles of feint, the months of Sunday school,
the gallons of free milk, all led to here:
an empty dining-car, a single fool
reflected endlessly on the night air.

11th February 1963

The worst winter for decades. In the freeze
some things get lost and I'm not even born,
but think until you're many Februaries
deep in thought with me and find London
on that day as held inside a glacier;
a fissure where two postal districts touch,
its people caught mid-floe, at furniture,
the contents of their stomachs, a stopped watch.
At these pressures the distance has collapsed:
the studio clock winds up over Primrose Hill,
or the poet and her sleeping children crossed
the mile to Abbey Road. This milk bottle
might hold what John'll drink for one last take;
that she'll leave out for when the children wake.

was the first book I owned, not counting annuals,
eighteen volumes of the *New Junior Encyclopaedia*
and an illustrated Bible. I could tick them off
as they occurred: so the starling, blackbird and house sparrow
fell on the first day, though the hoopoe and bee-eater
never blew through the 'wettest summer on record'.

Like a biroed Bede at his illuminations,
the pleasing lines of waders' beaks or raptors' talons
kept me occupied for hours. I wandered its pages
of saltmarsh, heath and scrub: it was its own landscape
and a codex to the calls that book-ended daylight,
becoming so revised and enlarged in the memory

that, sometimes, birds would bleed beyond their range maps;
so while the chough had pooled like glacial ink
in the Welsh hills, or the nightingale occupied that corner
of England left unscoured by the last Ice Age,
I half-heard a flinty *kwak* or the fluid phrasings
of 'one of our best singers' in a northern twilight.

How it came south I'll never know. A stowaway
in that first case I thumped onto puce candlewick,
camouflaged among the set-texts. I can entertain
the image of it making the round trip
back here, to the city it was printed in,
shedding its dust-jacket like juvenile plumage.

It seems smaller now, an index of wishful thinking.
Look at the notes in the flyleaves – the accidental visitors
and colourful migrations of one, bored summer –
offsetting the world outside my window, as if seen
down the wrong end of those field-glasses from Freemans
which were pawned for something irredeemable.

The Reading Hour

Placed under house arrest: a sentence long
as the Arctic tern's yearly flight, a straight ray
of arrowed light that left the sonorous
blues of an ocean trench and climbed
above sea-level, through giant sequoia,
Manhattan skyline, high as Everest
and cruising airliner. Let me play out
(he'd pray each evening, hearing the cries
of other kids) and live life in the quick
of bin-sheds and off-licences, moment
to moment; please abandon all hopes
for me, before the autumn term and rain
clear the streets; leave London's Underground
pressed in end-papers, and let me travel
no further than yourselves, my only pens
chained to post-office counters, or dangling
on string next to tomorrow's meeting-card.

Big Safe Themes

You can look all you like but the big safe themes are there
all around, forestalling what you were going to say.
A robust description of a cedarwood cigar box
has grown so big it could now contain Cuba and history.

No refuge in things. They stand at one or two removes
from the big themes; so any warm-weather fruit might bring
visiting times and the loved one we begged not to leave
as soon as you sniff at the rind or spit out a pip.

You can start with a washer, a throat lozenge, a mouse-mat
and watch them move in like the weather. Trying to be brave
ends in tears: I've seen the big safe themes walk all over
incest and morris dancing in their ten-league boots.

Why resist anyway? Bend with the big safe themes.
Let them do what they will and admit that the road you walk
again and again – right down to its screw-thread of blood
in a quivering phlegm – is becoming your big safe theme.

Cod

Those deep-sea fish had claims upon our souls.
What held the sense of mystery in our lives
like dark Good Fridays? Sometimes, if the rain
had slickened the streets into a Stanhope Forbes
and turned sandstone to pewter; if the forecast
gave more rain from the west for days on end
and warnings to the various fishing grounds,
we'd feel them close, a nuzzling all around,
the brush of barbels on causeways and piers,
their sea lanes washing into B-roads;
and, huddling in around our radios,
we'd trawl the bandwidths for a sign that soon
the sheet of cloud would break, the fish recede
back to the ocean cold from whence they came.

The Ages

The trees lay down their seam of coal as thin
as hammered gold leaf all afternoon
when a child is called in from the Iron Age war
he's been waging with the next street; road-works reach
the water table by teatime then knock off
for the day; late sun catches the last post
being emptied from an Edwardian pillar box,
warms the sleeping sandstone in its vertical dream;
there is a low Vent-Axian hum round the backs
of buildings, the usual insect holocaust
on filaments and coils; that hardening of the heart
that steals up on us like an early frost.

The ages, coming thick and fast tonight.
I caught one on my bedroom ceiling: the globe
of a paper light-shade caught in headlights
was a Golden Age symbol of truth and reason;
then a cold planet again. I yawn and fear the dark
like any good caveman. The buzzing that disturbs
my sleep might be a moth, or just the Creation
doing its thing on the skyline. I lie awake
in the blue chill, listening to the last teenagers
passing the house, their cries in the ever-after.

Dead Fish

Remember how they made us play Dead Fish?
If it rained, the dinner-ladies kept us in
and we cleared the canteen of its chairs and tables.
Have you forgotten how we lay so still?
The smell of old varnish, salt on the parquet,
or how the first five minutes were the easiest?
You'd find an attitude that you were sure
could last until the bell. Foetal, recovery:
each had his favourite. I'd strike a simple
flat-on-back, arms-by-my-sides figure
and concentrate.

                         Some fell asleep,
easy after seconds of tapioca,
and this proved fatal. Sleep is seldom still.
Others could last as long as pins and needles
allowed, or until they couldn't frame
the energies of being six years old:
some thought would find its way into a limb
and give the game away. But you were good,
so good you always won, so never saw
this lunch-time slaughter of the innocents
from where we sat out on the bean-bagged margin.
Dead fish in uniform, oblivious
to dinner-ladies' sticks poking their ribs,
still wash up on my mind's floor when it rains
in school hours. Blink if you remember this.

The Landing Stage

I've got this noise in my head: background or bedrock
is the best I can do for now. I've brought you here
to see if any of this might do the trick

like the tape of a favourite song or voice, familiar
and played in the hope the sleeper will awake
from a spell. I haven't been back here for years

and it takes a while to realise we're afloat;
the gangway down to the landing-stage is steep
at low tide. I'm hoping the river's moods and play of light

might kindle a sentence, or raise you from the deep
and empty stare that gives nothing back. I've brought
you to this exact spot, better to make the leap.

You know those hostages blindfolded in a boot
who memorise each bump in the road, the scent of tarmac
where a road opens up; who retrace their lost route

through its peals and toll-gates? This is how I get it back:
in pieces, the tang of a dream you can't forget
so carry around all day. Some proof: in this photograph

I'm listening under a pram's hood; against the sea-wall
a wind whips up your hair, a bottle blonde
I must have tugged a thousand times but can't recall;

gulls blur; the superstructures of Laird's stand
over the water, the brake is fast against the pram-wheel,
a curlicue of smoke rises, and for a split-second

I guess what story you were reading there. She knows,
looking up from her picture-book microcopy,
caught in a long vowel sound. Though the shutter was slow

the grey river hides its tons of cadmium and mercury.
The arteries harden and little by little the flow
stops. Oxygen-sensitive memory.

They say the deepest strata are slowest to fade,
so maybe you wander somewhere earlier, lost
in that job straight out of school, still learning to thread

the bobbin and foot, the samplers you ran off, the tests:
like a fern in a split coal, cracked open like code,
so the light of old afternoons can shine out of the past

and who knows what survives us. On that first five o'clock
in the machine-shop – the air revved up, a smell
of lint and sweat – the supervisor raised your work

and declared, 'Looks like you've done this all your life, girl . . . ':
so a chance remark in the light of forty years back
lives on in other minds; and you had so much to tell

which makes this silence harder. I can stand here and say
anything fluently now, to a woman in a wheelchair
who read to me, who took time out of those days

that must have contained so many things – newspaper
under a maiden strung with drip-drying nappies,
kindling in the grate, buttery fire-lighters –

and even though this stranger knows the little good
it does, talking into the wind; that his words are gone
before you know it; that you hear only collapsed chords,

I'll tell you how corncrakes have been heard again
out on the Isle of Man; how it's being said
that salmon are jumping the Howley Weir above Warrington;

that the grey river recalls each note and will reel them off
like verb forms taught by rote. The river remembers
its whiting, fluke and mackerel well enough

and their counterpoint that sounds in the shell of our ears
and moves in from the west, that peak and trough
and roil of surf which is our cantus firmus.

An Erratic

This glacial boulder weighs nearly a ton.
Its parent group is Cumberland volcanic.
After aeons it was moved by sheet ice
to the Mersey basin. In 1908
the City Engineer placed it here
in front of Wavertree District Library,
behind these black railings, a 'meteorite'
to generations of schoolchildren since.
Some still run their fingers round its surface
but its work here is done: any magnetic
properties have dimmed with age, and so
it essays now in scruple and endurance.
Somewhere inside the lending library
you'll find it mentioned by George Harrison
in his book I Me Mine *(where he also*
praises the quality of Liverpool water,
as fine as any he'd known for washing hair,
so altering the course of popular culture).

Establishing Shot

It might as well come here as anywhere.
Pick any card: street-lamps, tall leylandii,
rotated ryegrass in available light.
A long, slow take. Half-closing day. No one
playing out. A goal-mouth chalked on brick
is a frame within a frame just for a moment
before the artless pan resumes: bollards
and gutter-grass; and those who've just dipped in
expecting wide-screen, a lone rider
descending from high plains; the sans serifs
of Hollywood, strong language from the outset
or a director's trademark opening
will want their money back. We may as well
admit this is THE END too, while we're here.

The National in Exile

(MANOD QUARRY, NORTH WALES)

You recognise the image in the image:
in black-and-white, they stand to either side
of Jan van Eyck's 'The Arnolfini Marriage'
like any tour group taken by their guide.
But what you took to be the gallery wall
is banded with the seams of solid rock;
those men are not your classic urbanites
either: boots mark them out for dirty work
and elements; those layers that they feel
the kind of cold you find at depths or heights.

Beyond the frame a wider picture spawns:
the steep path up through shale they always took,
waist deep through each lake of moonlit ferns
to a village in some radioless nook
of a valley, where other evacuees
are sleeping in a quiet they've never known,
their eyes led through a dream of hills and distance
that they will carry back to factory towns
with their little suitcases; the schools and galleries
emptied for the blackout and insurance,

the great halls stencilled with landscapes and portraits
of wallpaper; the light of history
packed up and carried underground in crates.
The masterpieces hang here on display
in this most private of views, where slatemasons
rotate El Greco, Turner and Seurat
because no-one is looking, because the gaze
of 1941 is like a searchlight
trained on the incendiary heavens.
Each must have his favourite: the blaze

of barred coal sunsets, an avenue
of trees, the traders driven from the temple . . .
They must take it in turns to guard them through
the night, knowing these angels that people
their dark world won't return in this life;
that the slate they cut will take its own Grand Tour
into a larger, worldly exhibition
that roofs Europe. But let your eye repair
outside all that, inside this photograph,
this match of hosts with atmospheric conditions.

I've taken to sitting on this side passing through here
because I'm falling in love with the glassworks. The driver
is smitten too: he slows down for this length of the track
and we open our minds to its mysteries; a yard in the back
where puddles are set in a slurry of gravel and silica,
the marine blues and greens of its chutes and bays, the exotica
these must lead into; its thousand degrees, its extrusions
and alchemy. And as usual the syrup-forms harden
into words for a moment, and though I can't speak for the driver,
flashing by in no particular order
come David Bowie squashed flat on the cover of *Lodger*;
the crack I made playing in Solon Street with my first caser;
the way Harry Worth found the right angle, bifurcated
himself, and, using his own reflection, levitated;
the glazier gag, an offshoot of the invisible rope trick;
dark origins of 'daylight robbery' and rectangles of brick;
whatever it was/is between the snow and the huge roses;
the lump of N5 that came crashing through in the small hours;
the copper climbing through when we thought we'd been abandoned;
Lewis's, Boodles, T. J. Hughes, Blacklers, Ethel Austin;
the floors of tour boats and the clarity of the Aegean;
the roof of a grotto beneath a tench pond in a garden;
the slow molten myth of the thickness towards old sills;
betting my dole on the square, arched or round of *Play School*;
the Kitemarks of sea level that toughen at depths or heights;
the piece on my Airfix 1/25 *Spirit of St. Louis* I couldn't fit;
sashes and port-holes and skylights and transoms and screens;

pebbled and wired and tinted, vessels or vitrines;
sharp for a moment then running like rain on a window,
like this one (I sigh like a lover) I'm looking through now.

Joseph Beuys

To write about elemental things, to render
the world in its simpler smells and shapes and textures,
to describe how tallow collects under the finger-

nails, how felt feels against bare skin
is not, I repeat, not an option
having lived several times removed from the world as itself,

although it can do no harm to imagine
myself as the stricken airman
carted indoors by the local women

who'd take it in turns attending to the matter
of rubbing in the Stork SB and Flora,
the Golden Churn and I Can't Believe It's Not Butter.

For the House Sparrow, in Decline

Your numbers fall and it's tempting to think
you're deserting our suburbs and estates
like your cousins at Pompeii; that when you return
to bathe in dust and build your nests again
in a roofless world where no one hears your *cheeps*,
only a starling's modem mimicry
will remind you of how you once supplied
the incidental music of our lives.

Winter Hill

The transmitter stands lonely in my mind,
remote and cold, beyond the aerials
of gable-ends and guttering, beyond
ideas of Eiffels casting silvery bolts;

remote as the front that brought snowfall
to *The Undersea World of Jacques Cousteau*;
apologies from high on distant Pennines,
though something of a signal still gets through.

Metropole

When thunder woke us, moving up the Channel
in the early hours, the room stifling,
you wondered why it's always reassuring,
a storm heard from bed, the blue-pink flashes
that must have ushered in most of our summers
with their simple concepts: positive, negative,
five seconds for each mile between the lightning
and its report, the building up of static;

and cool and warm chalk clashed on two blackboards
a few miles apart as we compared
old notes, lying there: the balloon and hair-brush,
the hail in cloud 'like popcorn, like bingo balls';
and it turned out both of us had volunteered
to stand before the class and spread our palms
on the Van de Graaff generator's sphere
as the physics teacher cranked, raising our hair

and cracking up the lesson. We laughed in bed
remembering some distant afternoon
we both thought we'd forgotten – drawn together
by the force of memory – attracting paperclips,
our skin tingling for hours. Say both things happened
on exactly the same day, and after school
we'd met – say at some bus-stop or the ice rink –
and brushed against each other. What then?

I posited. Here was my grand theory,
my celebration of uncertainty,
my 'send champagne on ice up to our room',
signed in as 'sisters' was it that evening?
Hadn't everything we'd seen and heard since childhood
worn away the easy, black and white
world we'd been born into? I could hear
the beach between my questions, hissing shingle.

Even lightning itself. Hadn't they captured
the image of a kind of counterbolt
leaving the earth, leaping from tree or steeple
to meet the cloud? I waited for some answers
but none were forthcoming, so I listened further,
counting back to where each flash had issued
in super-cells beyond imagining
far out at sea, and drifted back to darkness.

A Tunnel

A tunnel, unexpected. The carriage lights
we didn't notice weren't on prove their point
and a summer's day is cancelled out, its greens
and scattered blue, forgotten in an instant

that lasts the width of a down, level to level,
a blink in *London to Brighton in Four Minutes*
that dampens mobiles – conversations end
mid-sentence, before speakers can say

'. . . a tunnel' – and the train fills with the sound
of itself, the rattle of rolling stock amplified,
and in the windows' flue a tool-shed scent,
metal on metal, a points-flash photograph,

and inside all of this a thought is clattering
in a skull inside the train inside the tunnel
inside great folds of time, like a cube of chalk
in a puncture-repair tin at a roadside

on a summer day like the one we'll re-enter
at any moment, please, at any moment.
Voices are waiting at the other end
to pick up where we left off. 'It was a tunnel . . . '

Diary Moon

You are the plainest moon. Forget all others:
shivering in pools, or spoken to when drunk,
that great Romantic gaze of youth; shed all
sonatas, harvests, Junes, and think instead
of how your phases turn here in a diary:
stripped of sunlight, surface noise and seas
you move unnoticed through the months, a bare limn
achieving ink blackness, emptying again.

You who turned inside the week-to-view
my father carried round each year, past crosses
that symbolized pay days, final demands;
in girlfriends', where red novae marked the dates
they were 'due on', and I shouldn't've been looking;
who even showed in weighty Filofaxes,
peeping through the clouds of missed appointments,
arrivals and departures, names and numbers.

On nights like these, which of us needs reminding
to set an eel-trap, open up the bomb doors
or sail out of the harbour on a spring-tide?
What sway do you hold over our affairs?
Although for some you're all that's there, printed
across the white weeks until New Year;
moving towards windows that will not frame us,
into the evenings of our sons and daughters.

The Sea in the Seventeenth Century

God's foot upon the treadle of the loom,
the sea goes about its business.
The photogenic reefs of the Pacific
can build for an eternity before
the cameras come, the kelp-forested shelves
of cooler waters absorb the wrecks
that scour their beds, a hint of the drift-net.
Ocean life goes on as usual, though.
A pulsing, absolute state of affairs
where all our yesteryears go through the lives
we might still live. It's boring in a way,
like heaven. Good Friday, 1649:
the first elvers have gained the estuaries
of Europe; a generation of spider crabs
are wiped out by a crustacean virus;
box jellyfish are deserting the shores
of a yet-to-be uncovered continent.
You'd almost think, nature being nature,
there would be some excitement at the trace
of poison from the Severn; at one part
night soil to the billionth of Thames:
that sightings of the brass-helmeted diver
would start a murmuring that God is dead.

The Message

Up early, hard at it,   the writer has paused
for his breakfast, a brace of   the finest Manx kippers
posted from Douglas   the previous evening,
packed into a horrible   soixante-neuf,
a Piscean rictus   pulled clear of a fire
regarding the writer   through four milky lenses.
He stops to consider   the plight of these herring:
their life in the deep grounds,   in sea-time, in numbers,
that couldn't have dreamt up   a drift net, a wet dock,
less still the sharp steel and   the dark of a smokehouse,
the surface mail franked   with an ocean's adieu:
an inky waveform.   He likes eating mail-food.
He likes its potential,   its margin for error:
the risks of a rupture   tainting a postroom,
or leaving an oyster   to open and wonder
null in the dark   of a cold pillar-box.
After he's finished   he's back at his keyboard
composing his latest,   imagining the scene
on the morning we log on,   discover his message,
and try to unravel   what's left of our data,
all raddled with glitches   like hair-bones in kipper meat;
to plug all the garbage   being fed down the phone-lines,
the effluent e-mails   that spoil and persist
like the stink of a kipper   in somebody's kitchen.
He hopes that we get it,   this mutable epic
that serves to remind us   we swim the same waters:
our spreadsheets all scrambled,   the wrong letters sent out,

the share points eroded,   the dormant account
suddenly flush,   the sad loss of three chapters
and even the poets   aren't getting off lightly.

Umbrella

I'm looking for a classical umbrella,
the kind Freud dreamt of, newly evolved
from walking-stick, before it lost its ferrule
or gained a fancy telescopic action.

I'm not interested in going so far back
as parasol or bondgrace, or lurching
sideways into Crusoe's skin and bones
contraption, or the lean-tos of antiquity.

No. I want the deeper, bat-wing pitch
that swarms and darkens streets in rainy footage;
a stick with weight and heft – hickory perhaps –
that lightens when its canopy is raised,

cut from a cloth that blocks out light as sure
as camera capes or courthouse head-blankets;
that, taut, could envelop the listener's head
and amplify the racket from a cloudburst.

Eight spokes, the heavens carved up into zones.
Italian work, the black Strad of umbrellas.
I'm still looking, soaked to the skin outside
an importer of handmade fetish wear.

The Barber's Lull

Unwinding from my crown, a weather system
of hair, anticyclonic since a birthroom
howl of laughter at the dark mohican
I was issued with. I've watched him work his way

clockwise about the cow's-licks and the split-ends
of my youth, and now can feel him closing in
as he does around the ears; sense his scissors'
ticking screw-pin, granular snicks.

We go eyeball to eyeball for the fringe:
he wins, then takes a step back, has a look
at his work, then looks again in the big mirror
at the two of us, looking; and though my mind

is elsewhere – underground in fact, picturing
my long bones set like jewels into a pad
of grave-hair – I sanction him, the first word
that's passed between us since I took his chair.

He's been doing me so long it's all unspoken.
I watch a nod begin in the nape mirror,
then step outside the ring of my own making
and sweep aside such thoughts, until the next time.

Sunspots

When the solar physicist declares
'the sun is now halfway through its life'

it seems to me as if the sun knows naught
of shadows or time; just huge, cyclical flares

we've latched on to sometimes: as Andeans
waiting for the pock-faced god's return;

as woodcut skaters moving through each freeze
in the minimums of Maunder, Wolf and Oort;

an eleven-year-old surfing the short-wave band
in his pyjamas, lost in all the noise.

Relic

One's a crown, two's a crown,
three, four, five distal occlusal,
six distal occlusal, seven occlusal.
Upper left: one mesial incisal,
two mesial incisal, three's a crown,
four, five is absent, space closed.
Six occlusal, seven occlusal, eight.
Lower left: one's a crown, two mesial,
three, four occlusal, five is absent,
space closed. Six occlusal, seven occlusal,
eight is absent. Right: one, two, three,
four distal occlusal, five's a buckle,
six and seven are absent, space closed.

Phone Books

You find them in the dark of meter cupboards,
in kitchen drawers, part of the scenery
left over from the last lot, like the sliver
of soap on the enamel, the flowery curtains.
They belong there, in the receding spaces
where somebody has turned from their unpacking,
looking to change the locks, to phone a curry
or just to thumb-flick through the Residential,
accepting its counsel of proportion
and scale: a city reduced to these pages.
A book you open somewhere in the middle
like cities themselves, like books of poetry.
Soon, this aerial photograph of print
has shape and contour – terraces of Smith
and Green, abutments of Honeycombe
and Read (see also Reed or Reid), exotica
in the columns of Q and X and Z – an atlas
drained of its delicate colours that offers up
the chance to find how many of our namesakes
are locked into its sequences, these districts.
Older editions, the ones that wandered
up into lofts, or down to sheds they share
with mildew and a Lucozade bottle
of weedkiller, the codes all changed, the numbers
decaying by the minute, gaining a power
to divert and transfix: before you know it
you're marrying the voices of childhood

(whose faces you forget) off to initials
and streets, streets where the rain gurgled from gutters
to grids you knew like birdsong, back-entries
which gave back a clean, metallic footfall,
or that kippered damp behind the weighted doors
of phone-boxes, their cracked vanity mirrors
and punished books, like this one . . . Time passes
in the fluid, eddying way that those absorbed
in words enjoy, until something rouses you –
that irruption into the old phone-box
back there, say; a tea-ring, or a number
circled in pen that tears the register
right down the middle like mail-order muscle –
and brings the afternoon back, those curtains,
a plane going over and the grainy silence
of an empty room. Singular and plural,
they lie there blank as any *tabula rasa*,
but can yield up multitudes. Out-of-work actors,
sometimes we find ourselves sitting on boxes
reading from the phone book, to nobody.

Peter and the Dyke

He's in there still, with Johnny Appleseed,
with all the frogs and sleeping princesses
but won't budge. I've tempted him with liquorice,
with pipe tobacco and Dutch magazines.
This is dedication, a child's endurance.
Outside, the longshore drift of my late teens
and pull of every tide that's turned since
are as nothing to his freezing fingertip.

Negatives

Years after the chemist we hold them aloft
to see if all is right in that other world:
this sliver of a snowy strand at midnight,
its rocky outcrop molten in dark sea,
and in its lee an aunt emerging from
a black beach-towel, pupal and six years old

again. Your mother builds an ice-palace
and stares back radiantly as if her soul
is burning to escape; everyone frames
an inner light, even the men who've found
a half-decent alehouse and stand soot-faced
at a long bar of porcelain and glass,
glamorous in silver tuxedos.

We have to handle negatives carefully
the envelopes say as we slide them back
in paper frosted up like lounge-bar glass,
like ice knocked from a pond, the middle key
we sometimes find unchanged and by itself
on hot afternoons; that has no negative.

Monkfish

Fishmongers, with an eye on trade,
will usually take the head
clean off, and offer up the tail
on slopes of oily piste instead.

A waste. Eyes that have known a dark
so absolute deserve this kind
of afterlife in ours; to look
upon this kingdom of the blind.

Memento mori in Waitrose.
A skull dropped in my parka hood
by John the Grave, who terrorized
the Liverpool of my childhood.

Thorns

I saw it all sharply again at a thousand feet,
above the tree-line, my eye being drawn
away from The Lion and the Lamb, coming to rest
on the solitary black mass of a thorn
growing out of grey rock;
or my ear was led by the song-flight
of a shrike on its way to the nest:
either way I was hooked.

It looked like a mould of the veins of the heart,
a fright-wig, a land-mine under a dugout
stilled by a shutter, depending on where I stood;
it was crooked at an angle, set
firm as if in the face of a gale
even on the calmest day, in one mind, alert
should one of those 'worst blizzards
in living memory' come over the hill.

A bush fitted with its own weapon system.
I approached it the way you would
a Burryman, his arms outstretched for a burr-hug,
or a porcupine ready to draw blood.
The Biblical ur-plant, twisted to its core,
knotted and fibrous, each wizened stem
carrying code out to its furthest twig.
I'd seen the like of all of this before:

they planted thorn in the Groves and Brows and Folds
we moved out to in 1971
and it thrived, above and beyond
the caged saplings, the windbreaks of pine,
old beech shedding its mast onto concrete
and dying slowly in streetlight. Its stranglehold
was absolute and everywhere you'd find
great brakes and stands of it.

I look back on that time as into a thorn bush:
never some easy flashback,
more a tangle to be handled with due care.
Speared among the larder of the shrike
I imagined the wrappers of extant/extinct brands,
unspooled cassette tape, a cash-till cartouche,
all snagged on the hardy perennial of my childhood years.
I moved in with my hands

past a house-sparrow – a *spadger* – airlifted up
from some lowland estate
by the butcher-bird, which brought to mind
some early lore: when budgies headed straight
from their cages for open windows, to fly
out into that world, they'd manage one aerial lap
before the scrambled spadgers found
their range and locked on. From a slate-grey sky

there'd be a snowfall of bright feathers
as if angels were having a pillow-fight.
Branches fork and meet, twist and snarl
the way fiction and fact collude and clot,
drawing blood and attention.
I follow one. It leads to my grandfather,
who lived just long enough to see us go decimal
and move out twenty stops to 'that midden',

only here he's a soldier again on the Western Front
caught on one inch of the millions of kilometres of wire
that coiled through his stories: Arras, Amiens,
Ypres. A teenage Volunteer
feeling the wind turning volte-face,
and from across the salient
the first whiff of phosgene.
He pisses on a handkerchief and covers his face

and I lose his features to the twisting thorn,
mediaeval in its methods of war
and the best defence for a sleeping Ladybird princess.
I helped build such a zareba
myself once; wove thistle, bramble and nettle
to fortify and hold onto a back-field den,
to keep out the shite-hawks of Halewood, Speke and Widnes.
Helix of carpet-tacks, staples and BCG needles

I could spike pages from that world up like receipts:
The Observer's Book of Birds' Eggs,
the *Edge* westerns, Ed McBain and Sven Hassell,
the works of Herbert (Frank and James), *Street Drugs,*
The Joy of Sex I doubt anyone shared,
Papillon, with its butterfly-and-rusty-padlock conceit,
the *Pan Book of Horror* series, the Bible,
The Valley of the Dolls and *The Thorn Birds.*

I could get my wires crossed and hear my mother
whacking the ganglion that grew in her wrist
with our bible, the Freemans catalogue
or the phone book, whichever was heaviest;
could hear the air-brakes of buses bound for town,
the grudging *alright*'s between shift workers
below my window, the barking of great-grand-dogs,
and a voice I'm sure was my own:

by now, the bush had started to look
like a sprinter coming out of the blocks
or as if it were about to jump
like an angry hill god, or a Jack-from-a-box.
The blood must have drained from my face: body-clock
and mountain time seemed to be stuck,
bringing another world to life and I felt a lump
harden in my throat as the bush spoke:

Remember me? I know I'm looking rough.
It's me, you silly cunt: you if you'd stayed
back there until the bulldozers moved in.
I'm everything you might but never made
of yourself, a man stripped to his fighting weight.
I'm what you like to think you've shaken off,
though every place you've ever been since then
has seen something of me along the way.

Even here – walking in the English Lakes! –
they'll meet the prickly pear, the spiky fucker
beneath the surface, as you see me here.
The years have been cruel to you, old mucker;
turned you shite-soft, your sharp edges to mush.
See how I've still got everything it takes
to hang on, while you've drank a lake of beer
and toked so much you could turn into a bush!

All his soft tissues eaten away.
I wanted to point the finger, to blame someone,
to turn this bush into a voodoo doll
reversed out; so I could impale Lubetkin
and Luftwaffe; the faceless councillors
and aldermen who gave the nod one day
decades ago; all those I thought accountable
dangling in an aquatint by Goya.

But finding such an image of myself
in such an unlikely place
left little room for blame, and the sap
soon dropped. Surprising myself, I said to his face:
'The two of us both wanted the same thing
once. Many's the time we've taken off
out of the hardness, going way past our stop
into the sticks and breaking into song

as townee dreck tend to when on the move,
littering the sides of public roads.
It's happened here before: a girl from Manchester
left proof, a few sorry words
at the door of a two hundred years old journal;
or the discharged soldier, still seen from a grove
of 'thick hawthorn', in verse, not far from here.
Though by and large they've become invisible.'

The teenage me kept shtumm, inscrutable
and bush-like again on these matters,
and a softness rose in me thinking of him
failing to make his mark, and all the others
who grew up in those unraked Zen gardens
among the bonsai thorn, the babble
of television on in the daytime;
and if this were a vision, then here it ends

with a man stood shivering at a thousand feet.
My speech is still a thorny, north-west stew;
I walk along each public right-of-way
a trespasser; there is no single view
worth taking; rootless man, still clinging on
to some idea of truth, some ideal state
just round the next bend, found out today
he's bound towards a republic of thorns,

the flag it flies: straining, grey polythene;
its rhyme and scheme, the way it founds a voice;
its bird-life, clinging to an older way;
the way it soldiers on and knows its place.
The wind picked up. And so I left the thorn
abiding there, and dropped onto the green
and soft floor of an easygoing valley,
imagining I could start from scratch again.

Jingle

To say we shelve the adverts somewhere safe
is to say the shite we put into the sea
has no bearing upon this earthly life . . .
He slipped in stuff like this while writing copy.

Gibraltar

It suits me down to the ground, the idea
of living on that rock, where the grey Atlantic
meets the Med, and the streets all wind down
to the sea; where they keep a decent Guinness
and the pubs are open all day. Who would I be?

I'd be an ex-pat, a career criminal
doing time in the sun before admitting
there's nowhere left to run; I'd be a waster
selling timeshare; but mostly I would be

a twitcher, living for the spring and autumn,
when all the birds of Europe are on the move,
and we could be the stillness in the heart of
all things, me and the rock, watching the swallows
bound for where the sex-lines terminate.

Fly

Hardly anything, a fine-winged fly on the window pane,
one of the day's ten thousand seconds captured,
made visible. Inconsequential, its moments in the world
squandered on this wall of light it can't surmount,

far from water. It must have got in overnight
through one of those chinks we don't like to admit
to owning – with our campaigns of strip blinds, Insect-o-cutors
and arsenic paper, you could say we haven't got on,

that you remind us of something we'd rather forget;
some thread of trial and error, intricate
and long since perfected, fully working before we arrived
on the scene at one minute to midnight; that you knew

summers of the smaller hours, Venusian seasons
and still go through the whole thing on bus-shelter roofs,
canals, anywhere warm or wet enough. Can you see me –
a castellated, bloodshot eye, day's growth –

and did you see me enter, or feel the slammed air
then a settling through the house, silence again
and onwards in your slow ascent from the sill
against the dawn's skin, gorged a red that you see in waves.

Up close, you've spat on your hands, that same solving rub
when faced with sashes, great bays, or top decks of buses
the world over, baffled in our era of glass
that you slip against time and again, *en route* for an edge

though it's strange the way you'll so readily accept a frame,
tracing an algebra of infinite confinement,
a treatise on the lack of straight lines in nature,
that hard-bitten philosophy found in cage birds

and aquaria; a pattern I've seen displayed
on skylights, shithouse walls, the pelts of dead dogs;
or trapped in famine footage, a matte blip
that kept Lindbergh awake as he crossed the Atlantic

again in the late film. The east has grown bright.
In your register of time, I have held this pose
steadily for hours. In mine, all I have to say
is brushed to one side as I give up writing this,

take a fly-age to cross the room, draw back the lace;
to lift up the latch, encourage you with one sharp breath,
the air catching your wings, letting noun become verb,
and you join the world of things, of everything being the case.

An Interior

They ask why I still bother coming back.
London must be great this time of year.
I'm not listening. My eyes have found
the draining-board, its dull mineral shine,
the spice rack, still exactly how I left it,
knives, a Vermeer vinyl table-mat.
How many hours did I spend watching
the woman pouring milk into a bowl
that never fills? I never tired of it.
Vision persists, doesn't admit the breaks
the artist must have taken, leg-stretching
alongside a canal twitching with sky
not unlike the leaden one outside;
or just leant on the door jamb, looking out
onto a courtyard, smoking a pipe
before going in, to sleep on his excitement.

Surtsey

Someday I'll make the trip via Icelandair
then boat to Surtsey, to stake a claim
on an island that was still active the year
I was born; a toe-hold in the North Atlantic
being photographed from planes for future terms
in distant Comprehensives. I could walk

that same dark coastline we watched thrown up
in Geography; its lava lakes, lagoons
and fountains cooled to a concrete townscape;
could spread a palm against its walls and floors
like kids who climbed the apron to feel the screen
for warmth; could catch that same trace of sulphur

we caught on a Widnes wind; could carry the words
we learned then – *magma, pumice, rivulet* –
back to source, and see how well the birds
have done since a pair of gulls in sixty-eight;
or how a cruciform of sea rocket
has bloomed beyond the classroom's colour plates

and flourished like the grasses in the play-scheme.
I'd find what else its first habitants have left:
a breeze-block ruin some scientist called home;
the Portaloos of vulcanologists;
spend Surtsian nights far from the red-shift
of streetlight, knowing it still exists

on the edge of memory. The cameras
have gone. I used to kid myself on cold
evenings walking home from school, and wonder
in the quiet after such a difficult birth;
the cries of sea-birds leaving me old
beyond my years in the youngest place on earth.